MAKE IT FROM NATURE

Everyone's going back to Nature! And it's fun and easy to create special things for special people—all from Mother Nature's treasure house.

From a pretty pebble, seeds and grains that you find along the roadside, acorns or pine cones from a walk in the woods, driftwood or sea shells from a visit to the shore, you can make natural jewelry, Christmas tree ornaments, a really different lamp, or even a shocking pink spinach-eater!

Be creative—the natural way.

MOTHER NATURE'S CRAFTS BOOK

By ALEXANDRA EAMES OLMAN

Illustrations by Lauren Rosen

PYRAMID BOOKS ▲ **NEW YORK**

MOTHER NATURE'S CRAFTS BOOK
A PYRAMID BOOK

Copyright © 1975 by Alexandra Eames Olman

Pyramid edition published January 1975

ISBN 0-515-03570-X

Library of Congress Catalog Card Number: 74-15280

Printed in the United States of America

Pyramid Books are published by Pyramid Communications, Inc. Its trademarks, consisting of the word "Pyramid" and the portrayal of a pyramid, are registered in the United States Patent Office.

Pyramid Communications, Inc.
919 Third Avenue, New York, N.Y. 10022

CONTENTS

INTRODUCTION

Save those rocks and shells! Here are some great ideas for things to make from old camp collections gathering dust in the attic or just those sticks and pretty leaves gathered on a country walk.

The materials for all the projects are Nature's own, but even if you live in a city we show you where to find them—in the fish store, the pet shop, the florist's and the supermarket. Anyone anywhere can make sand or dirt drawings, try leaf decorating and pressed flower pictures, make a lamp full of beans, or design seed ornaments for the Christmas tree.

We show you how and Nature makes it easy. You'll have all the fun!

TOOLS AND MATERIALS

Here is a list of all the tools and materials whose names you might find unfamiliar. If you can't find a certain item in your store, don't be afraid to ask for something else that might do the job just as well for you.

DUCO CEMENT
A strong glue that comes in a tube; it's flexible, waterproof, and dries clear.

WHITE HOUSEHOLD GLUE
Elmer's or Sobo glue that comes in a plastic bottle, can be mixed and thinned with water, is white when wet but dries clear.

RUBBER CEMENT
A clear glue that comes in a jar or can with a brush applicator used for temporary gluing. When dry it can be rubbed off any surface easily with your finger. Also used for dry mounting for permanent gluing.

PLIERS THAT CUT WIRE

Sometimes called jeweler's pliers or, in the hardware store, diagonal pliers.

METAL WIRE

Wire can be copper, aluminum, or even real silver or gold. Look for it in variety stores, hardware stores, jewelry supply stores, or hobby shops.

ROSE STAPLES

Usually used to attach rose branches to a trellis or garden fence, they are U-shaped nails with a point at each end. You can buy them in hardware stores.

FINDINGS

Backings for rings, pins, earrings, clasps, and all other materials used in jewelry making. Look for them in variety stores or hobby shops.

AWL

Looks like an ice pick and has a sharp point for punching holes. Buy it in the hardware store.

ACRYLIC PAINT

An acrylic polymer paint that comes in a tube or a jar and mixes with water. When it dries it becomes waterproof. Wash out brushes in water before the paint dries or let them sit in a jar of water while you work.

LIQUID PLASTIC

A plastic or polyurethane varnish to protect and add gloss to almost any material. It comes in a matte (or non-shiny) as well as a glossy finish. In our projects we refer to the glossy finish only. Wash out brushes with household ammonia. There are also acrylic varnishes; brushes used with these can be washed with water.

POSTER BOARD, MAT BOARD, ILLUSTRATION BOARD

All are colored cardboard found in art supply stores. Poster board has a smooth surface. Mat board is heavier with a slight texture and is most often used as a border around pictures inside the picture frame. Illustration board is a heavy cardboard made for illustration or drawing.

CHAPTER I

ROCKS AND PEBBLES

Rocks and pebbles are almost everywhere you walk. At the seashore or along a stream, rocks are smooth and round. In the mountains you will find jagged gray stones or even quartz, which is white or pink and very sparkly. Somewhere you might even find a good-luck stone— a black stone with a white stripe running through it. Look for big rocks for the doorstop or bookends and lots of tiny pebbles for the planter. If you live in a city and don't have a vacant lot with stones or pebbles, try a pet store for fish-tank gravel, a florist, or the plant department of a variety store.

PEBBLE PLANTER

Decorate a plain plastic flowerpot with tiny pebbles to give an indoor plant the Natural look. Use a small pot because a large one will get too heavy.

You need: 1 plastic flowerpot about 4 inches in diameter, lots of pebbles (about the size of peas), Duco or other strong cement.

How to Make:

1. Wash all the pebbles in a bucket of soap and water and then spread them on newspaper to dry. Wash the pot if it's dirty and dry it well.

2. Turn the pot upside down. Glue a row of pebbles around the edge of the rim. The rim will give them something to rest on so they don't slip off. Let the glue dry.

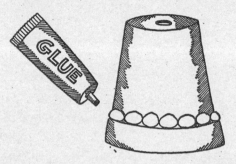

3. Glue another row of pebbles above the first row. These can rest against the first row of pebbles. Let the glue dry.

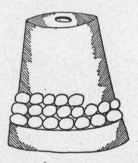

4. Glue on more rows until this part of the pot is covered.
5. With the pot still upside down, glue rows of pebbles around the rim in the same way until it is covered.

6. Now you are ready to plant! Put a few pebbles in the bottom of the pot, add some soil, and then your seed or a plant that is already growing. Water it well and see what happens!

ROCK-PILE SCULPTURE

There is no special design for making rock-pile sculpture. Look for interesting rocks in strange shapes or use lots of small plain round stones. When you make your sculpture you can make it tall or wide, fat or skinny, but try not to make it so heavy you can't lift it!

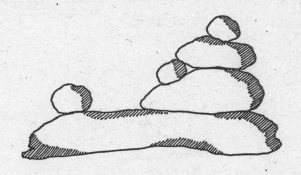

You need: An assortment of rocks in different sizes, Duco or other strong cement, liquid plastic (optional), a square of felt the same size as the bottom of your sculpture.

How to Make:

1. Wash the rocks in soap and water and let them dry on a sheet of newspaper. If there is dirt in the cracks, use an old toothbrush to scrub them.

2. Start with your biggest rock. This will be the base of your sculpture. Glue another rock onto it. You have to pick the one that you think looks good. Let the glue set. If a rock starts to fall off before the glue dries, prop your sculpture up against a book or lay it on its side to hold them together.

3. Add rocks wherever they look nice. Check out the balance of your sculpture after each rock is added so you know it will stand up. It's like playing Blockhead, the balancing game!

4. Brush on a coat of liquid plastic if you want your sculpture to look shiny.
5. Place your finished sculpture on the square of felt and trace around the bottom with a pencil. Cut out the piece of felt and glue it to the bottom of the sculpture. This will keep it from scratching a table top.

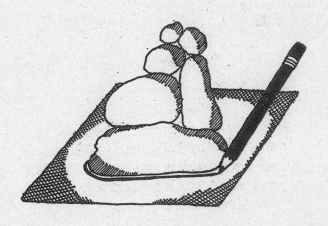

PEBBLE PENDANT

Make a plain old pebble into a pretty pendant to hang around your neck or dangle from a bracelet or pin. A coat of liquid plastic will bring out the color and make the stone bright and shiny!

You need: Small smooth stone in any shape, flexible metal wire, liquid plastic, brush, small pliers or wire cutters (try to borrow these), macramé cord, rawhide shoelace or chain necklace or bracelet.

How to Make:

1. Wash the stone in soap and water to be sure it's clean.
2. Brush liquid plastic on your stone and let it dry.

3. Cut off about a foot of wire. If your stone is very large, you may need a longer piece. In one end of the wire make a loop large enough to thread your cord, rawhide, or chain through.

4. Place the loop at the top of the stone and wrap the wire around the stone in a circle. Bring the wire back to the loop and wrap it once around the loop. See our picture.

5. Circle the wire around the stone again, crossing the first circle at a right angle. Wrap the end of the wire around the loop on top a couple of times and make it tight. Cut off any extra wire. (See drawing on next page.)

6. To make sure the stone won't loosen and slip out of the wire add a little cement under the loop and at the bottom where the wire crossed itself.

7. Now your pendant is finished. String it onto silky macramé cord, a silvery chain, or a piece of rawhide. You can find rawhide where it is sold as shoelaces for hiking boots. Or use yarn, ribbon, or even plain old string.

PAINTED ROCK CREATURES

Wild and woolly rock creatures are fun to make and fun to give to friends. They can be real—like ladybugs, turtles, or fish; or make-believe —like a shocking pink spinach-eater! Different shapes of rocks suggest different types of creatures. Fat, round ones make good ladybugs, while long, jagged ones make terrific dragons.

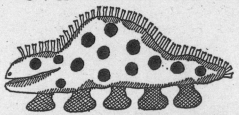

You need: A rock, acrylic paint, brush, plastic cup of water, liquid plastic, brush, Duco cement or other strong cement, yarn, feathers, pipe cleaners, string, felt—any assortment of things to trim your creature with.

How to Make:

    1. Wash your rock in soap and water and scrub it with an old toothbrush to get all the dirt off. Dry it well.

21

2. Look at your rock carefully and decide what you want to paint on it. You might see the eyes of your creature, or maybe a crack is really the creature's mouth.

3. Brush on the paint. Do one color at a time, letting each color dry thoroughly before you add the next color so they don't run together. For example, if you're doing a ladybug, paint her red first. Then add the black dots after the red has dried.

4. When the paint is completely dry, brush on a coat of liquid plastic. Let it dry.

5. To add a fringe of yarn hair, whiskers, or antennae, use the Duco cement. Pieces of macaroni and little pebbles can be glued on to decorate your creature. A small rock glued to a large round one makes the head of a turtle. Cutouts of felt can be glued on to make good feet, tails, ears and even tongues! Have fun!

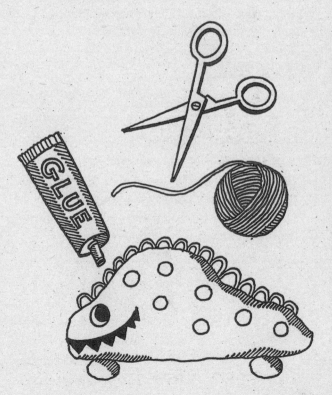

PEBBLE-COVERED KNICKKNACK BOX

Any little old box can become a conversation piece when covered in tiny pebbles. Maybe you'll find a discarded jewelry case that you can dress up as a knickknack box for yourself, or a music box that needs redecorating. If you collect pebbles in different colors, you can work out some fancy designs.

You need: Wooden or plastic box with hinged or separate lid, enamel spray paint (white, black, tan, or dark brown go best with pebbles), lots of pebbles about the size of peas, Duco or other strong cement, liquid plastic, brush.

How to Make:
1. If the box you are decorating is unfinished or badly scratched, or if you don't like the decorations on it, spray-paint it. Let it dry thoroughly.
2. Trace the shape of your box on a piece of paper. Arrange your pebbles within

24

this outline to see how your pebble design will work. Maybe you will want to make a border like the one shown, or maybe a center design (see picture).

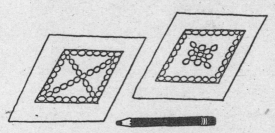

Keep pushing the pebbles around until you have found a design you like.

3. Transfer the pebbles to the top of the box, gluing each one in the same place it was in your design on the paper. If the pebbles wiggle too much and push each other out of line, wait until the cement has dried before you glue on more pebbles.

4. When all the pebbles are glued on and the cement has dried, brush a coat of liquid plastic over the whole box. It will help keep the pebbles glued down and makes them nice and shiny.

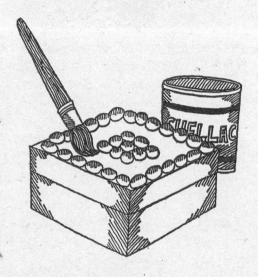

DECORATING WITH ROCKS

One large rock becomes a doorstop, two become bookends, and three small ones can be a set of paperweights. These are really easy and fun to make. You can leave the rocks plain, in their natural state, or you can paint them in wild patterns. If your doorstop turns out to look really artistic, you can put it on a table and call it sculpture!

You need: 1 heavy rock about the size of a brick for the doorstop, 2 for bookends, 2 or 3 small rocks for the paperweights, square of felt slightly larger than the bottom of each rock, Duco or other strong cement. If you wish to paint and varnish your rocks, you will need acrylic paint and liquid plastic.

How to Make:

1. Wash the rocks with soap and water and scrub off dirt with an old toothbrush. Dry them well.

2. If you plan to paint your rocks, do one color at a time. Let each color dry

27

before you add the next. The design can be stripes or dots or flowers, or personalized with initials.

3. When the paint is completely dry, brush on a coat of liquid plastic. Let it dry.
4. Place each rock on a piece of felt and trace around the bottom with a pencil. Cut out the pieces of felt and glue them to the bottoms of the rocks. This will keep them from scratching the surfaces you put them on.

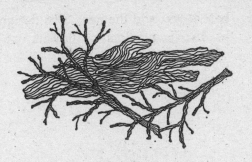

CHAPTER II

BRANCHES, STICKS, AND TWIGS

The next time you go on a picnic, or just on your way home from school, you can collect fallen branches and twigs for the projects in this chapter. Dead branches work best, and these are the ones you'll find most easily on the ground—and you'll be cleaning up the environment at the same time.

You can use branches or twigs with the bark on or off, depending on how you want your project to look. Sometimes the bark peels off easily and sometimes not. If the wood has dried out, the bark will flake off. If the branch is still green, soak it in water to make the bark softer and peel it off with a blunt knife. If you are working with a branch that has lots of little twigs, you'll find it very hard to remove the bark, so leave it in its natural state.

29

RIBBON BRANCH OR JEWELRY RACK

Nature grows a branch to hold up leaves. You can use it the same way, as a rack to hold all your hair ribbons, yarn ties, scarves, pendants, or strings of beads.

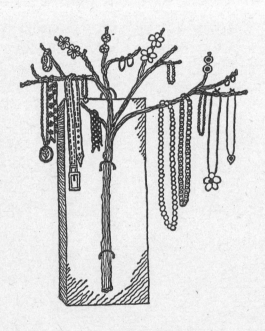

You need: A branch with several smaller branches still attached, a block of wood 8 inches long by 3 inches wide by ¾ inch thick, 3 U-shaped rose staples, hammer, scissors, spray paint (optional).

How to Make:

1. Start with a fairly big branch and then trim it. Snip off any little twigs that would break under the weight of a ribbon or string of beads. If a twig is so long that it bends down when you hang something on it, make it shorter.

2. If you wish, you can spray-paint your branch white or a color that goes with your room. Or you can leave it natural, to bring the outdoor look indoors. Paint the block of wood to match or leave unfinished.

3. Hammer one of the staples into the top of the block of wood. This will give you a loop to hang it from.

4. Lay the branch lengthwise on the wooden block. Place the other two

staples over the branch, as we show in our picture, and hammer them into the block of wood.

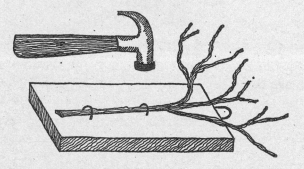

5. Hang the branch rack on a small nail in the wall and festoon it with all sorts of goodies!

BIRD'S NEST BASKET

This little basket is made almost the way birds make their nests, except that we use glue. Make one to put a potted plant in or add some dried grass to nest a collection of colored eggs. To make a nice gift, fill your basket with those little candies that look like speckled bird's eggs.

You need: A pile of twigs with the bark still on, tube of Duco cement.

How to Make:
1. Break a twig into 6 equal-size pieces about 2 to 3 inches long.
2. Lay the pieces in a circle on a tabletop covered with newspapers. Overlap the ends of the twigs and put a glob of glue wherever the twigs touch each other. Let the glue dry.

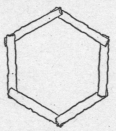

3. To make the bottom of the basket, break a twig into 6 shorter pieces and lay them around the edges of your ring. The ends of these twigs should touch the centers of the twigs in your first ring, so the layers are staggered. Glue the twigs in place.

4. Make the next ring with even smaller twigs; glue and let dry. Then add a few twigs across the smallest ring to form the bottom of the basket. Glue them in place and let dry.

5. Turn the basket over and add twigs to make the sides higher, laying on a ring of twigs and gluing them in place. As you build up the sides, you can make

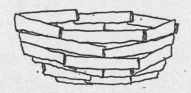

the rings larger by adding longer twigs. It's much easier if you let the glue dry after you add each layer.

6. Your nest can have lots of gaps between the twigs, or you can fill in with smaller twigs. Stick smaller pieces into these spaces and secure them with a spot of glue.

TREE SCULPTURE

Bring the outdoors in with a miniature landscape for your dresser or desk. A tiny branch becomes a tree in a mini-mountain of clay.

You need: A small branch in a windswept shape, about 1 foot tall with lots of twigs on it, moist clay (the kind that hardens, not oil-based clay), several rocks or pebbles, Duco cement, liquid plastic, brush, scissors.

How to Make:
1. Trim your branch into a pleasing shape if Nature hasn't done it already. Cut off any bent or broken twigs.
2. Form the clay into a mound that looks like a hill and make some gullies and grooves in it. Stick the branch into the clay and then take a couple of the rocks and press them into the clay and lift them out again. When the clay dries and hardens, you can glue the rocks into these spots permanently.
3. Let the clay dry. This may take several days.
4. The clay shrinks when it dries, so the branch may be stuck in tight. If it is loose, take it out and dab glue on the end and stick it back in the hole. Glue on the stones or rocks.
5. For a glossy finish you can paint the base with liquid plastic.

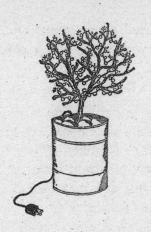

BRANCH TABLE LAMP

You have seen bare trees all dressed up at Christmas time with tiny white lights. Here's the same idea for your room at home. It won't be bright enough for reading, but it's great for mood lighting.

You need: A large branch, about 3 feet tall, whose twigs are strong enough to hold a string of tiny lights, 1 string of small Christmas lights, 1 gallon-size tin can, white spray paint (optional), several heavy rocks, extension cord 3 feet or longer.

Note: If you want to paint your branch white, buy lights that have a white wire; if you plan to leave your branch natural, get the green-wired lights.

How to Make:

1. Spray-paint the can and branch if you wish.
2. Place the end of the branch in the can and wedge the rocks in around it to hold the branch upright and straight. The rocks will also weight the can and keep it from falling over.

3. Arrange the string of lights over the branch so the bulbs are evenly spread out.
4. Plug the end of the light cord into the extension cord and carefully push the plugs down into the can and out of sight. Arrange the extension cord so that it falls behind the can. Plug the extension cord into the nearest outlet.

CHAPTER III

NUTS AND NUTSHELLS

Whether you collect nuts from under a tree or
buy them at the nearest supermarket, you are
sure to find lots of variety. In the woods there
are acorns from oak trees, hickory nuts, butter-
nuts, and horse chestnuts. In the store you will
find pecans, walnuts, filberts or hazelnuts, al-
monds, and, of course, peanuts. They all have
different shapes and colors and make exciting
and interesting projects—as well as delicious
snacks.

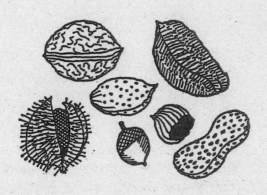

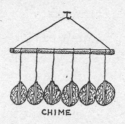

CHIME

WALNUT WIND CHIMES OR MOBILE

Here is a chime to hang on a porch or in an open window. When the wind blows, the empty walnut shells will gently bump together, making a soft, hollow sound. By making it a little differently you end up with a handsome mobile.

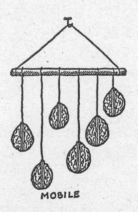

MOBILE

You need: 6 walnuts in their shells, a wooden stick about 10 inches long, nylon fishing line (the almost-invisible kind), white household glue, old blunt knife with rounded tip, scissors, paper clips.

How to Make:

1. Pry the walnut shells open with the blunt knife. Try to make them come apart along the seam; don't crack the shells. Take out the meat and eat it or save it for nut brownies!

2. Cut off six lengths of fishing line, each 18 inches long. Tie one end of each piece to a paper clip.

3. Place the paper clip inside half a walnut shell. Then glue the two halves of the shell together. Do this for all 6 walnuts.

41

4. Tie the walnuts to the stick about 1 inch apart, allowing them to hang down about 7 inches. To make the wind chime, keep all the walnuts level so they will knock together.

5. To make a mobile, stagger the walnuts so they hang on different lengths of fishing line.

6. To hang your chime or mobile, cut off about 2 or 3 feet of fishing line and tie each end to an end of the stick. Then hang it from a thumbtack or cup hook.

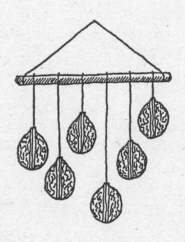

WALNUT SHELL SAILBOATS

Everyone makes these little boats just because
it's fun. Here are some ideas for fancying them
up with different kinds of sails and making
them into a decorative centerpiece. To celebrate
Columbus Day you might want to make three
boats—to represent the Nina, the Pinta, and
the Santa Maria.

You need: Some walnuts (each walnut makes
two boats), oil-base modeling clay (the
kind that doesn't dry out or harden),
white or colored paper, wooden toothpicks, scissors, blunt knife with rounded
tip, Duco or other strong cement, piece of
driftwood or small log with bark on it.

How to Make:

1. Pry the walnut shells open with the
   blunt knife. Try to make them come apart

43

along the seam, without cracking the shell. Take out the meat and eat it!

2. Roll a little ball of clay and press it into the center of the shell.

3. Cut out your sails from the piece of paper. If you are a serious sailor, you can make your sails in real nautical shapes. The Marconi rig has a triangular sail; the gaff rig has a triangular sail with the top cut off; the square rig has a square sail (just like Columbus's ships). Or you can make a really crazy sail, shaped like a flower! (See these shapes in our pictures.)

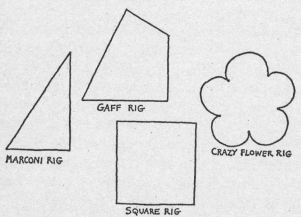

MARCONI RIG

GAFF RIG

SQUARE RIG

CRAZY FLOWER RIG

4. Push the toothpick through the paper sail and stick the end of the toothpick into the lump of clay inside the walnut shell.

5. Glue the boats, in sailing formation, to the driftwood or bark-covered log.

ACORN DOOR PLAQUE OR SIGN

Acorns are little nuts that come from oak trees. When they are ripe they are brown, and the caps—the top part that looks like a hat—easily separate from the acorns. Little kids often pretend that the caps are saucers and the acorns are cups—great for their miniature tea parties! Whole acorns can be glued to a sign or plaque for decoration. Arrange them in little clusters or in rows. A sign with a family name makes the perfect gift for a neighbor or friend. And if you can't find acorns, use other nuts.

You need: Lots of acorns that are ripe and brown, a piece of wood about 5 inches wide by 10 inches long (oak is especially nice, but you can use other wood as well), pencil, brown acrylic paint, Duco or other strong cement, small paintbrush, sandpaper, liquid plastic and a brush, sheet of carbon paper.

How to Make:

1. Sand the rough edges of the wood and sand off any dirty spots.
2. Plan your sign. For example, look at the designs above. One is done in script and the other is printed in block letters. On a piece of paper draw or write the name the same size you want it to be on your sign. Go over it until it looks right. Then place the carbon paper, ink side down, on the piece of wood and put the paper with the name on it on

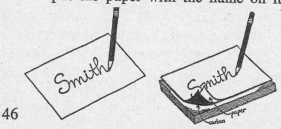

top of the carbon. Trace lightly over the name with a pencil. Try not to lean heavily on the paper because the carbon might smudge and leave ink on the wood.

3. Now paint on the name with a small paintbrush, following the lines left by the carbon paper. Let the paint dry.

4. You're ready to decorate the sign with acorns. Glue them on with the cement in clusters or as a border, mixed with other nuts. Let the glue dry until it is hard.

5. Brush on a coat of liquid plastic. Let it dry for several hours or overnight, then give it another coat. This will make the sign weatherproof so it can be hung outdoors.

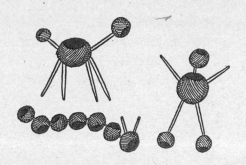

HORSE CHESTNUT PEOPLE AND ANIMALS

If you have a horse chestnut tree growing near you, you'll find lots of nuts to make a whole world of people and animals. The horse chestnuts grow on the tree inside a very prickly shell. When the chestnuts become ripe in the fall, they drop off the tree and the prickly shell opens up. Inside it is a very glossy nut in a beautiful brown color. The kind of chestnuts you eat are called Italian chestnuts, but you can't eat horse chestnuts.

You need: Horse chestnuts in different sizes, wooden toothpicks (the round kind with sharp pointed ends), a sharp darning needle or a sharp nail.

How to Make:
    1. Pick the horse chestnuts for your animal. Use a large one for the body and a smaller one for the head.

2. Attach the head to the body by pushing a toothpick into the chestnut. Then attach a smaller chestnut to the other end of the toothpick. Sometimes the chestnut is too hard for the toothpick to go in; then you need to make a little hole in the shell with the needle or nail to get the toothpick started—the inside of the chestnut is soft. If the toothpick is too long, pull it out, break off a piece, and push it back into the chestnut.

3. Attach chestnuts and toothpicks until you have the right shape. See our pictures for lots of ideas.

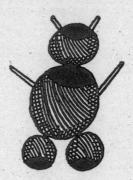

NUTSHELL ART

If you've collected a lot of different kinds of nuts, you can work them into an unusual "picture." Your design can include real things—a house, a car, people, flowers—or it can just be a pattern of lines and swirls. It's the variety of nuts that makes it look and feel different from other kinds of art.

You need: Assortment of nuts, piece of wood about 1 foot square (this can be plywood or pine from the lumber yard; ask the lumberman if he can sell you a piece from his scrap pile), liquid plastic, brush, Duco or other strong cement, sandpaper.

How to Make:

1. Sand the rough edges of the piece of wood. If there are any dirty spots, sand them off.
2. Spread all the nuts out on a tray. Then place them on your board to try out the design you are thinking of. Push them around to see how they will look.

50

3. With Duco cement glue the nuts in
   place. If you find your arm bumping
   some of the glued nuts out of place, let
   the glue dry before adding more. You
   can leave some open spaces for the
   wood background to show through or
   cover it all with nuts.

4. When the glue is completely dry and
   hard, brush on a coat of shellac or
   liquid plastic to give it a nice shiny
   finish.

CHAPTER IV

SEA SHELLS

Whether you find sea shells by the seashore or in the fish store, you'll have plenty to choose from. By the Atlantic Ocean you find scallops, clams, snails, and mussels. Along the Gulf coast of Florida are tiny little shells called coquinas, which come in lots of beautiful colors —pink, lavender, yellow, orange—and can be scooped up by the handful. If you have any relatives or friends who live in Florida, you might ask them to send you some coquinas.

If you don't live near the ocean, look in a fish store for different varieties of clams, oysters, and mussels. You can feast first and then save the shells for these projects! Jewelry, sculpture, and frames made from shells are so popular these days you can make them for gifts or even sell them—and make a profit!

SHELL NECKLACES

Hang a pretty shell on a chain, on a piece of rawhide or ribbon, or on a metal circle that goes around your neck. We show several designs, but your ideas may be even better! You will need those little metal rings, about the size of a pea, to hold your shell jewelry together. They're called findings and are sold in hobby or notions stores.

SCALLOPS

MUSSELS

You need: Shells in different sizes, hammer, awl (a sharp pointed tool that looks like an icepick), findings (metal rings—if you can't find them in a store, take them off old or broken costume jewelry), small pliers, package of wooden beads, liquid plastic, brush.

How to Make:

1. Clean the shells in soap and water.
2. Using the awl and the hammer, punch a hole in the edge of the shell (as we show in the picture). Do this over a small piece of wood to protect the table top. It will take only two or three gentle taps with the hammer. Make the hole close enough to the edge so the metal ring will fit into it. If you plan to attach two shells to each other, make holes on each side, or on the top and bottom.

3. Brush a coat of liquid plastic on the shells to make them colorful and shiny. Before it dries be sure the hole is open and not clogged with plastic.
4. Slip the open end of the metal ring into the hole in the shell. If you plan to attach the shell to a link in a chain necklace or to another shell, slip the other end of the ring through it and then squeeze it closed with the pliers.

5. A single shell can be slipped on a piece of ribbon or rawhide and worn as a pendant. Or you can string it on and then add several beads on either side and then add two more shells. Dream up any combination! See our pictures for ideas showing the shells attached lengthwise, making a long pendant, or side by side, making a choker or belt.

SCALLOPS

EARRINGS, RINGS, AND PINS

These are all very easy to make. You can buy
the findings (the earring backs, pin backs, and
plain rings that you can glue decorations onto)
in a hobby shop or notions department, or re-
cycle them from old costume jewelry. If your
beach hasn't produced any exotic-looking little
shells, try a novelty shop where they sell
bunches of shells in little plastic bags.

RING   EARRINGS   PIN

You need: Shells, findings, Duco or other strong
         cement, little pearls or colored beads,
         liquid plastic.

FINDINGS

RING   EARRING BACK   PIN BACK

How to Make:

1. Clean the shells in soap and water.
2. With the cement glue a large shell to the
   finding. Then add some pearls or beads
   or even smaller shells to decorate it.
   Sometimes one really pretty shell looks
   better all by itself, without any pearls or
   beads. Let the glue dry thoroughly.

3. Brush the shells and the top of the finding with a coat of liquid plastic. This will make them look shiny and help keep the shells stuck in place.

CLAM SHELL BUTTERFLY

Hang this butterfly from the ceiling in your room or let him sit on your desk as a paperweight or sculpture. Or you can make a whole flock of little ones to give to your friends.

You need: 2 clam shells that match each other, awl, hammer, flexible wire from a hobby shop, plier-type wire snippers, colored pipe cleaner, acrylic paint in pretty colors, small paintbrush, liquid plastic and brush, Duco or other strong cement, nylon fishing line or string (optional).

How to Make:
1. Clean the shells with soap and water and let them dry.

2. With the awl and hammer punch two holes on each side of the hinge on each shell.

3. Paint each shell like the wing of a butterfly. Make the shells match up as we show in our picture. Paint a bright color all over. When it is dry add stripes, dots, and patterns in other colors. If you are going to hang your butterfly so you can see the underside, paint that too.

4. When the paint is dry, brush on a coat of liquid plastic.

5. Cut off two 5-inch lengths of wire with the snippers. Loop the wire through the two holes and twist the ends together. Loop the other wire through the other two holes and twist the ends. Make these wires tight enough so the clam shells stick out sideways and your butterfly will look like it's flying.

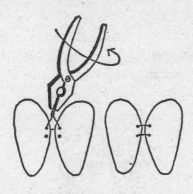

6. Bend the pipe cleaner into a *V* and curl the ends. This is the butterfly's antennae. Glue it on with cement.

59

7. Cut a 3-foot piece of nylon fishing line or string and tie each end to the wires holding the shells together. Then hang the butterfly from a nail or cup hook in the ceiling, where it will dangle freely. It will also look pretty just sitting on a shelf or your desk.

DECORATED MIRROR OR PICTURE FRAME

You can make any ordinary old picture or mirror frame beautiful and expensive-looking by gluing on sea shells. You see huge mirror frames

smothered with scallop shells in the fancy decorator shops and in magazines these days, but you can make your own—with any shells. Start with an unfinished wood frame and leave the shells in their natural colors or take an old painted frame, glue on the shells, and spray-paint the whole thing a gleaming white. Use only one kind of shell or a variety—the more the better!

You need: Shells, unfinished or painted frame about 2 inches wide, Duco or other strong cement, liquid plastic and brush, or spray paint.

How to Make:
1. Clean the shells in soap and water and let them dry.
2. Experiment by laying out the shells on the frame in a pleasing pattern. See our pictures for ideas.
3. Glue the shells in place with the cement. If the shells overlap each other, glue the

61

one underneath first and then glue on the others. Add little shells to fill in the gaps in your design.

4. If you like the natural look of the wood and shells, brush on a coat of liquid plastic or shellac. If your frame is an old one, spray-paint the whole thing, shells and all. Do several lightly sprayed coats to get good coverage without drips of paint.

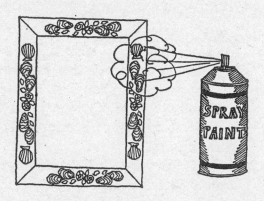

SHELL FLOWER PICTURES

Here is the ideal project for those coquina shells from Florida or pearly blue mussel shells from the fish store. The shells are arranged like the petals in a flower, so different shapes of shells can make different kinds of flowers. Make a shell flower picture to give someone for Christmas.

You need: Assortment of shells, tiny pearls or beads, 11-by-14-inch piece of colored poster or mat board, standard 11-by-14-inch picture frame without glass, Duco or other strong cement, green pipe cleaners.

How to Make:
1. Clean the shells with soap and water. If you are using mussels that have been steamed or cooked, soak them overnight to get all the meat off. It wouldn't be very good to make a fishy-smelling flower picture!
2. Brush a coat of liquid plastic on all your shells and let them dry.

3. Place the shells on the poster or mat board and arrange them in flower shapes (see our picture). Use long shells for the petals and a fat round shell or cluster of pearls or beads for the center. Lay out the pipe cleaners as stems and see how the picture looks.

4. Glue each shell and pipe cleaner in place.
5. When the glue has thoroughly dried, set the poster or mat board in the frame. Put the piece of cardboard that comes with the frame in the back of your picture and bend down the metal tabs that hold it in place.

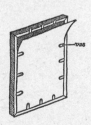

CHAPTER V

SEEDS, GRAINS, AND BEANS

Mother Nature produces all sorts of seeds, beans, and grains—in the woods, along roadsides, and in fields. Look for grains on the ends of stalks of ripened grass; seeds and beans in the pods of wildflowers after they've finished blooming. If Nature doesn't yield enough in your neighborhood, you can always go to the supermarket and buy various kinds of beans in different colors and shapes: black turtle beans, black-eyed peas and chick peas, red kidney beans, and green peas. They are all dried and come in plastic bags. Watermelons, squash, and pumpkins are full of beautiful seeds which you wash off and let dry for a few hours. Or you can buy mixed wild-bird seed. One bag will make lots of projects, and then you can feed the birds with the leftovers.

PILL BOTTLE SEED SCULPTURE .

It's the different textures and colors of seeds and beans that make this sculpture interesting to look at. Ask your family to save all clear plastic pill bottles. If everyone is really healthy and you can't get used pill bottles, try the five-and-ten for empty plastic containers. Import stores often carry nice square or rectangular plastic boxes.

You need: Lots of different seeds and beans or grains, empty pill bottles, Duco or other strong cement.

How to Make:

1. Wash out the pill bottles if they have been used before and dry them carefully.

2. Fill each bottle with a different kind of bean, seed, or grain and put the lid back on. If the lid is loose add a dab of cement to keep it shut.

3. Glue the bottles together in any pattern you can. The round bottles can go side

by side or one on top of another. The square boxes are best for stacking like a bunch of blocks. (See our pictures for some ideas.)

4. Once the glue has dried you can set your sculpture on a table or hang it on the wall.

BEAN AND SEED CHRISTMAS TREE ORNAMENTS

For a truly natural Christmas tree indoors, decorate it with these seed and bean ornaments. Combine them with lots of real pine cones and strings of popcorn, and the tree will be really beautiful.

You need: Lots of seeds, beans, and grains, Styrofoam balls, white household glue or Duco cement, pipe cleaners (optional), liquid plastic and brush.

How to Make:

1. If the Styrofoam ball does not have a hook to hang it with, put some glue on the end of the pipe cleaner and insert it into the Styrofoam. Let the glue dry.

2. Rest the Styrofoam ball on top of an empty can or glass to keep it from rolling

around. Spread a little glue on and add the seeds or beans. Arrange the seeds in rows or in patchwork sections—or any way at all! If you find you are knocking off the seeds you just put on, let one area dry before you begin the next.

3. Continue adding glue and seeds and beans until the whole ball is covered. Alternate rows of tiny seeds with sunflower seeds, or you can use rice to vary the texture.

4. When the glue is all dry, brush on a coat of liquid plastic to help hold the seeds and beans in place and to give the ornament a glossy finish. Let it rest on the glass or can until it's dry.

NATURAL NECKLACES AND BRACELETS

Using all the different types of beans and seeds, you can design a whole wardrobe of necklaces—chokers, long beads, or beads with pendants. Save squash and watermelon seeds in the summer, pumpkin seeds at Halloween.

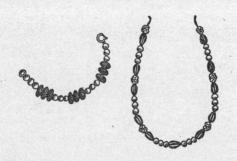

You need: Beans and seeds, needle and thread, glass of water, necklace clasp and ring (optional).

How to Make:

1. Soak the beans and seeds in the water for an hour or so or until they are soft enough to pierce with the needle. They may look wrinkly when they are wet but will smooth out again when they dry. Handle them gently so you don't tear the skin—that's the pretty part.

2. Thread the needle, double the thread, and knot the ends together. The thread should be the length you want your necklace to be, so measure it around your neck or wrist, making it just a bit longer.

3. Pierce a bean with the threaded needle and pull the thread through. Keep stringing beans or seeds on the thread in a pattern: for example, three green peas, two black turtle beans, three peas, two black beans, and so on. Stick in a few pumpkin or sunflower seeds for variety.

4. When you get near the end of the thread, remeasure your wrist or neck to be sure you have it right, and then knot the two ends of the thread together. The bracelet will have to be big enough to slip over

your hand, or you can add a clasp and ring to fasten it. Use the clasp, too, for choker necklaces. Before you cut off the thread, run the needle through the clasp several times and knot the thread.

5. To make a pendant to hang on a long string of beans or seeds, thread the needle with a short thread, string on a few large seeds, piercing the fat end of the seed, and then pull the thread into a tight circle. Knot both ends of the thread and tie the pendant to the long string of beans and seeds.

BOTTLE OF BEANS LAMP

Here's how to make a handsome lamp and re-cycle a large glass bottle at the same time. The bottle should be of clear glass — a big wine bottle will work fine, or a plain soda bottle without much lettering on it. Buy the electrical fixture at the hardware store. It has socket, cord, and plug all in one piece, together with a cork that fits right into the neck of the bottle. All you do is stick it in.

You need: Lots of beans (three or four different kinds), large clear glass bottle, electrical socket and cord with cork on the end, a plain clamp-on lampshade.

How to Make:

1. Soak the bottle in warm soapy water until the label peels off easily. Let the bottle dry thoroughly inside and out.
2. The beans should fill the bottle in layers. First pour in a couple of inches of one kind, then an inch or so of another kind. Make a cone-shaped funnel out of paper so the beans don't spill all over. Do not wiggle or move the bottle as you are pouring in the beans or they will get all mixed together. Keep adding layers all the way to the top of the bottle.

3. When the bottle is almost full, push down on the beans to pack them a bit more

tightly and then push the cork end of the socket into place. If it doesn't fit, pick out a few beans with tweezers.

4. Screw in a light bulb and clamp on the lampshade. Presto! The lamp is ready to be plugged in.

CHAPTER VI

LEAVES, FLOWERS, CORNHUSKS, AND PINE CONES

Wildflowers, weeds, and posies from the garden, as well as pine cones and cornhusks, are the raw materials you need for these creative ideas. Gather pine cones in the woods or ask the florist to order them for you. Corn on the cob is a summertime thing, but you can dry the husks and stow them away for midwinter projects.

PRESSED LEAF AND FLOWER COLLAGE

This takes time but not energy. The pressing can take as long as a month, so if you want to make a collage and then give it as a birthday gift, you will have to plan ahead! The only hard part is remembering a month later that you started the project in the first place! Use flat types of leaves and flowers, like clover, ferns, pansies, and daisies.

You need: Leaves and flowers in pretty shapes and colors, roll of paper towels, tweezers, picture frame with glass, colored cardboard or construction paper to fit the frame, cardboard backing for the frame, cellophane tape.

How to Make:

1. To press the leaves and flowers place them between two sheets of paper towel. Be sure they are lying flat and not over-lapping each other. Then place the towels between the pages of a big telephone directory, dictionary, or other heavy book. Stack a few more books on top.

2. For the first two days change the paper towels every eight hours. The paper will have absorbed most of the moisture in the leaves and flowers. Leave them in the book for about a month. When you go back to your project, the leaves and flowers will be paper thin but will still have their natural color.

3. To make the collage lay the colored paper or cardboard on top of the cardboard backing on a table. Then take your pressed leaves and flowers and lay them in a design. A natural bouquet shape is pretty. Use tweezers to pick them up, very carefully so they don't break and

fall apart. If the petals fall off the flowers, just put them back in position on the paper. Move the pieces around until you have the design just right.

4. It's best not to glue this kind of collage to the background because the glue might change the colors of the petals and leaves. Instead you will have to lay the glass from the frame on top of the leaves and flowers without moving them. Then squeeze all three layers together and tape them along the edges. This will hold them together as you slip them into the frame. If the collage fits loosely, add another piece of cardboard in the back to make it tight. Then fold the prongs of the frame down against the backing . . . and hang your picture on the wall!

LEAVES AND SPRAY PAINT DECORATING

Give a table top, chair back, headboard or even your lunch box a pretty leafy pattern. Or you can buy an inexpensive metal tray in the variety store, decorate it, and give it to someone as a Christmas, birthday, or thank-you gift. Leaves come in lots of shapes; maple, oak, and beech leaves, as well as ferns, are easy to find. In flower shops they have lemon leaves and ferns. Use the leaves while they are still flat and green, before they dry and curl.

You need: Leaves, rubber cement, spray paint in two colors (one light and one dark), liquid plastic, brush.

How to Make:

1. Spray-paint the object all over if it needs fresh paint. If you are doing a large piece of furniture, it's cheaper to use a brush and a can of paint. Let it dry thoroughly.
2. Lay the leaves at random or in a pattern on top of the object. If you are doing a

chair back or headboard, lay it on its back so the leaves don't fall off.

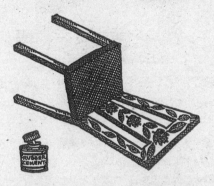

3. To keep the leaves from slipping or blowing out of place put a little spot of rubber cement on the back of each.
4. With the contrasting-color spray paint, spray lightly over and around the leaves. You can either do a solid coat covering all of the first color, or you can spray it in cloud-shaped areas just around the leaves.

5. Carefully lift off the leaves while the paint is still wet. Try not to smear the paint. Let the paint dry.

6. After the paint is completely dry, rub off the remaining spots of rubber cement with your finger.

7. Brush on a coat of varnish or liquid plastic. This is especially good for table tops or trays that need protection.

PINE-CONE CHRISTMAS WREATH AND MINIATURE TREE

Pine cones grow in almost every state of this country and come in all sizes, from the tiny ones that grow on the hemlock tree to the great big ones from the Ponderosa pine. They look especially beautiful used as decorations at Christmas time. We suggest you try a wreath or miniature tree, but use your imagination and you'll think of lots more things to make.

You need: Lots of pine cones in different sizes, Styrofoam forms (either in a wreath shape or a cone shape to make the tree), thin flexible wire (often called hobby wire), thin wooden sticks (available from florists), plier-type wire clippers, Duco cement or other strong cement.

How to Make:

1. Cut off a length of wire and wrap it around the pine cone. Since there are spaces between the scales, the wire can be pushed toward the center of the cone and out of sight. Twist the two ends of the wire together. If the cone is small and light, leave one strand of wire about an inch long after twisting the ends together. Cut the other end off. If the cone is heavy, it may need the support of both ends of the wire twisted together as a single strand. Wire each cone, doing as many as you think you'll need.

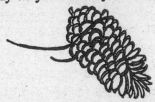

2. Insert the end of the wire into the Styrofoam. If it starts to pull out, add a drop

83

of glue behind the cone to stick it to the surface of the Styrofoam form. If the pine cone is very heavy, you may want to use a stronger wire. For big cones that won't stay stuck in the Styrofoam, wrap the wire around a piece of wood the size of a matchstick. Insert the wood into the Styrofoam.

3. For the wreath, put the biggest cones on first in clusters or in rows. Then add smaller ones to fill in the spaces in between. You could start with a cluster of large cones at the top of the wreath and fill in the rest with smaller ones.

4. For the tree, start with larger cones at the base and use the smaller ones as you work toward the top. Or just cover the whole thing with cones all one size.

5. To give the wreath or tree extra sparkle, wire a few tiny silver or gold Christmas balls and insert them among the pine cones. Or brush clear nail polish on the

tips of the scales of the cones and sprinkle on metallic glitter while the polish is still wet.

CORNHUSK DOLL

Here's a project that recycles the part of the corn that you usually throw away—the husks. They're the leaves that cover corn on the cob. You can also use the corn silk, that fluff that sticks out the end of the cob, as hair for the doll. So the next time you have corn on the cob for dinner, save the wrappers!

You need: Cornhusks and silk, scissors, string, bowl of water, white household glue.

How to Make:

1. After you peel the husks off the corn, they have to be dried. Do this by laying them out on newspaper in a warm, dry place, preferably in an open area where the air circulates. A dry hot attic is a good place, or near the furnace. This will take several days.

2. Once the husks are dry, they will be stiff and curled up. To make them soft and pliable keep them in the bowl of water while you are making the doll.

3. To make the doll's head and body, take five or six husks and tie them tightly with string about an inch down from the blunt ends. Trim off the corners of the husks to make a head shape. (See drawing.) Turn the bunch upside down and fold the husks down over the tied part. Pull them down smoothly and tie another piece of string around the neck.

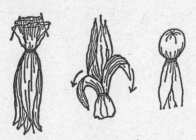

4. For the arms take three thin strips of husk, tie them together at one end, braid them, and tie the other end. This piece

should be about six inches long. Divide the husks that form the body in half, just below the neck, and slip the braided piece between them. Tie another piece of string around the body just under the braid and then loop it around the neck and tie it tight. (See drawing.)

5. Fold two husks lengthwise until they are each about an inch wide. Lay one over each shoulder, crisscross them in front and back, and then tie them down with a piece of string wound around the waist.

6. For the skirt you will need several wide husks. Lay them on the doll with the blunt ends just above the waist, and tie them with a piece of string. Then take another husk, fold it lengthwise and wrap it around the waist to cover up the string. Tie it on and then fold the top edge down over the string. While the skirt husks are still wet, you can arrange them in folds. When the husks dry, the folds become permanent.

7. Now, all your doll needs is a head of corn-silk hair. After the husks have dried, glue on the silk with white household glue, and top off her hairdo with a tiny straw flower.

CHAPTER VII

SANDS AND GRAVEL

Here are some good reasons to mess in the dirt and end up with something more lasting than mud pies. Even city folks can find sand, gravel, or good substitutes like potting soil, fish-tank gravel, or even kitty litter. In the suburbs you can dig up dirt and find sand by the side of the road—and that blue stone used for paving driveways works well too. Think about it for a minute and you'll come up with all sorts of material to work with.

SAND CASTING

Now you can preserve doodles in the sand forever or create interesting textured designs (called bas-reliefs by artists) to hang on the wall or sit on a table.

You need: A dishpan or baking pan of sand, some pretty rocks and shells, plaster of Paris, water, plastic bucket or pan to mix it in, stirring stick, wire (optional).

How to Make:

1. Sprinkle the sand with some water to make it damp enough to model. Scoop out a shape—a bird, face, anything! Then poke and scratch the surface of the scooped-out area to give it texture.

2. Add a few rocks or shells to your design and stick them part way into the sand.

3. Mix the plaster of Paris with water according to the directions on the package. It has to be smooth enough to pour easily. Pour it gently into your sand mold.

You may want to spoon in a little at first so as not to disturb the design.

4. If you plan to hang your sand casting, make a loop of wire and lay it in the wet plaster. Let the plaster set until completely hard.

5. Lift the hardened plaster out of the sand and brush off the loose sand. The remaining sand, shells, and stones give the plaster surface beautiful texture and color.

RAINBOW-STRIPED
BOTTLE ORNAMENTS

This is fun to make and fascinating to look at.
You can use clear pop bottles, jelly jars, any
clear glass container with a screw-on top, or a
wine bottle with a cork. The sands or gravel you
use can all be natural, in shades of tan and brown,
that you've dug from the ground, or they can be
in brilliant colors from the fish and pet store. Do
be careful with fish-tank gravel as it is often made
of glass chips and can cut your hands. Use a
scoop, a plastic cup, or a big spoon to handle it.

You need: Two or more kinds of sand and gravel,
clear glass container with a lid, something
to scoop it with, spray paint (optional).

How to Make:

1. Scoop up and pour a layer of one color
of sand into the glass container. (If
the neck of the container is narrow
make a paper funnel so you don't spill
sand all over.) Make this layer at least

½ inch deep. The layers that go on top can be heavy and will pack down the bottom layer. Tilt the container so the sand ends up deeper on one side. That way the layers above will look nice and wavy.

2. Set the container on a table and pour in the second layer in a different color. Try not to tilt or jiggle the container and pour the sand very gently so you don't disturb the layer underneath.

3. Keep adding layers in different colors until you reach the top.

4. If you wish, you can spray-paint the lid a bright color. After it dries, put the lid on the bottle—and that's it! Display your sculpture on your desk or dresser or give it to someone else to enjoy.

SAND AND DIRT DRAWINGS

If you are into the Natural look, you'll love these easy-to-make "art works." You can either use all one type of sand or dirt or mix different kinds and colors. Beach sand is pale beige, potting soil is dark brown, clay soil is often gray or rusty red. A variety of textures can also make your drawings more interesting—use fine sand for part of the drawing and pebbles for another area.

You need: Sand, dirt, or gravel, a piece of cardboard (this can be gray shirt cardboard or plain white or colored poster or illustration board), white household glue in container with painted spout.

How to Make:

1. You can either draw your design directly with the glue, or you can draw the design in pencil and then trace over it with glue. Vary the line of the glue, making it thick and then thin. Make swirls or

geometric shapes or whatever pops into your head. If you are doing a very large drawing, do one area at a time so the glue doesn't dry.

2. Right away, while the glue is wet, sprinkle on the sand or dirt. Pick up the cardboard and shake it so the sand covers all the wet glue. Don't touch or smudge the glue once the sand is on it. Just let it sit and dry, and then shake off the extra sand.

3. To mix different kinds of dirt and sand, do one area with one kind, then let it

dry and shake it off before you do the other kind of sand or dirt.

4. If you want to fill in flat areas with sand, spread the glue as you spread mayonnaise, in a smooth even layer. Then sprinkle on the sand. If there is extra sand let it sit on the glue until the glue dries, then shake it off.

5. Frame your finished sand drawing in a simple wood frame from the five-and-ten. If there are lots of big pebbles in your drawing, take the glass out of the frame. If you have made a really big drawing, buy a wooden stretcher (the kind used for oil paintings) without the canvas and glue the cardboard to the face of the stretcher. This will keep the cardboard from curling and make it easy to hang.